TRI-CHEVY LEGEND
THREE GOLDEN YEARS

TRI-CHEVY LEGEND

THREE GOLDEN YEARS

Mike Key

Acknowledgements

I would like to thank everyone who helped me in obtaining the photographs for this book, particularly all those people who took time out to allow me to photograph their cars – without them, there would be no book.

Thanks, also, to the Classic Chevy Club of America, and to David Bates Travel for making all the travel arrangements for my trip to the USA.

All the photographs were taken on Fujichrome RDP 135 film, using a Nikon FA and a range of lenses. The pictures were processed by Reflections of Norwich.

Chevrolet™ and Chevy™ are registered trademarks of the General Motors Corporation.

First published in Great Britain in 1994 by Osprey, an imprint of Reed Consumer Books Limited, Michelin House, 81 Fulham Road, London SW3 6RB and Auckland, Melbourne, Singapore and Toronto

© Mike Key

ISBN 1 85532 422 9

Editor Shaun Barrington
Page design by Reg Wright/Ward Peacock Partnership
Printed in Hong Kong

Half-title page
The changing face of the classic Chevy: 1955 – a clean, uncluttered design; 1956 – the first facelift with more brightwork and a full-width grille; 1957 – the final update with elaborate bumper and even more sparkle

Title page
Fins from the fifties: Chevy tailpiece from 1957

Right
Just a few of the automobiles that turned up at the Classic Chevy Convention in Oklahoma City – acres of fins and chome

For a catalogue of all books published by Osprey Automotive please write to:

The Marketing Department, Reed Consumer Books, 1st Floor, Michelin House, 81 Fulham Road, London SW3 6RB

Introduction

The years 1953 and 1954 were trying for Chevrolet, indeed as they were for other US car manufacturers, come to that. For several years after World War 2, the company had become used to selling just about every car they could make to a public that had been starved of new cars during the war years. But by 1953, the boot was on the other foot – buyers had become far more choosy and at the end of that year there were still a lot of unsold 1953 models. To make way for the new year's models, dealers offloaded their old stock onto used car dealers, who promptly discounted them, further stemming the demand for new cars.

For Chevrolet, locked into its annual production battle with Ford, times were particularly hard, for Ford was aggressively trying to grab the mantle of biggest manufacturer away from Chevy and was rolling cars out of the factory at an incredible pace regardless of whether its dealers wanted them or not. Who actually won the race in 1954 is debatable, for both manufacturers claimed the title, but it would seem that Ford actually sold a handful more of their 1954 models to the public than Chevy did.

For a long time, Chevrolet had been known for producing good, solid, dependable cars, which was why they sold so many, but they were none too exciting – the kind of cars that mom and pop and grandpa and grandma drove, but not exactly calculated to appeal to those of a younger frame of mind. The youth market had long belonged to Ford and its flathead V8 engine. Furthermore, by 1954, Chevrolet's products were getting a little long in the tooth, both in appearance and mechanically.

Chevrolet had three series of passenger cars on offer: One-Fifty, Two-Ten and Bel Air, all being based on the same body shell, the rounded lines of which could be traced directly from Chevy's 1949 models which, in turn, had been the company's first new post-war design. All were powered by the trusty, old, 235 cubic inch 'Blue Flame' six-cylinder engine, an overhead-valve design of pre-war origin. The One-Fifty models were at the bottom of the range, and the Bel Airs at the top.

So, as 1955 came into view, Chevy appeared to be in a spot. They were being pressed hard by Ford, they were losing out on the youth market, and they had a glut of new 'old' cars that weren't moving. It was time for a change and, fortunately, a change was coming.

Chevy had long envied Ford its dominance of the youth market, and for some time the company had been working on a new car that would take that dominance away. As 1954 came to a close, that new car would make its debut. It would be all new: a new body design and an exciting new engine (although the trusty 'Blue Flame' six would still be offered as an option for some time to come). Furthermore, it would be the first of a trio of what were to become 'classic' Chevies, recognised as something special at the time and still regarded so today. The 'hot one' was about to arrive …

Right
Open up! Classic Chevy owners love to lift the hood, which invariably reveals a pristine engine bay

Contents

1955: The Hot One arrives

In November 1954, amid a blaze of publicity, Chevrolet announced its redesigned One-Fifty, Two-Ten and Bel Air models for 1955. All had the same basic bodyshell and were hailed as the 'Motoramic Chevy', after General Motors' annual Motorama shows at which new models and styling prototypes were shown to a car-hungry public. But the '55 Chevy also carried another name, guaranteed to appeal to the youth market and particularly apt given its new, powerful V8 engine and subsequent competition successes – 'The Hot One'.

Compared to previous models, the '55 was all new in appearance; the rounded, tall-looking bodies of the past had given way to a squarer, wider and lower-looking version. The hood and tops of the front fenders were level; there were no longer any vestiges of separate rear fenders; the trunk lid and tops of the rear fenders were also level; while clever styling of the windows and roof produced a lower roofline. A dip in the beltline, just behind the front doors, also helped in producing the lower, longer look that Chevy stylists had set out to achieve.

One controversial aspect of the design was the grille. To a public used to wide, chromium-plated, toothy 'grins' on the fronts of their cars, the '55 Chevy's simple, rectangular 'egg crate' was radical to say the least. It received considerable criticism in the press, not least because of the difficulty in keeping it clean. With hindsight, however, it can be seen as a masterpiece of design, perfectly in keeping with the simple, but stylish lines of the car, lines that were to become somewhat blurred in the following two years.

Chevy had engineered a whole new chassis for 1955, preferring to stick to this form of manufacture, even though European manufacturers were moving into unitary construction, whereby a reinforced floorpan took the place of a separate chassis. Chevy's example had stout box-section side members and a massive X-member in the centre.

Right
The '55 Chevy had a classic simplicity of design that received much acclaim when it appeared. But the 'egg crate' grille was not always welcomed, being difficult to keep clean. With hindsight, though, it is difficult to imagine what else would have looked right. This very clean example of a Bel Air convertible belongs to Lance Denton who hails from Texas

Right

The classic Chevies have a strong following in many parts of the world, not just the US. Terry Peters' Bel Air sport coupe lives in England where it has had a starring role on TV and in the movie Buddy's Song. Essentially stock, but for the American Racing wire wheels and a 283 cubic inch engine instead of the original 265, the hard top shows the clean lines of the '55

At the front there was independent suspension with unequal-length wishbones and coil springs containing telescopic shock absorbers. Steering was provided by a box of the recirculating ball-type. At the rear, for the first time, a Salisbury-type axle with an open propshaft took the place of previous models' torque tube drive and banjo-type rear end. The axle was suspended on parallel leaf springs and controlled by telescopic shock absorbers.

Mechanically, however, the really exciting news was Chevy's new 265 cubic inch V8 engine. Available in all three series of cars, it was a winner from the start, being lightweight, efficiently designed and powerful.

Among the interesting features of the engine was the rocker arm arrangement, which dispensed with common rocker shafts for each bank

Above
The two-tone paint treatment offered on the Bel Air can be seen to advantage in this shot of Terry's sport coupe. The trim on the rear fender provides a neat split between the colours. An alternative two-tone scheme was available in which the roof was a contrasting colour to the rest of the bodywork

Left
Nice interior in Terry Peters' coupe. Note the dashboard trim, which was punched with hundreds of Chevy 'bow-ties' as standard. The shifter and pode-mounted tachometer are definitely non-stock, however

of cylinders. Instead, each rocker pivoted on a fulcrum at the top of a post pressed into the head; a locknut secured the rocker in place and provided a means of setting the valve adjustment. The rockers themselves were interesting too, being sheet-metal stampings rather than castings. The five-main-bearing engine had a bore and stroke of 3 × 3 inches.

In standard form, the new V8 produced 162 bhp gross at 4400 rpm, but an optional four-barrel Rochester carburettor and dual exhausts (replacing the normal two-barrel carb and single exhaust) lifted that figure to 180 bhp at 4600 rpm. Quite an improvement compared to the

Above
The Two-Ten series was the middle range of classic Chevies, and here is a very nice example of a Two-Ten two-door sedan. Note the 'Chevrolet' script on the front fender and lack of front fender 'spear', which was exclusive to the Bel Air. The Two-Ten also had less stainless steel trim round the side windows

Left
Kenneth Koch's four-door Bel Air sedan shows the alternative two-tone paint treatment. Note how there is no vertical trim between the rear fender 'spear' and bumper, as there is no need to split the colours at that point. Bright trims on sill and rear of front fender opening were optional extras

Above

Possibly one of the most sought after models of classic Chevy is the Nomad station wagon, complete with sports coupe styling from a Corvette-inspired show car. The '55 Nomad is probably the most attractive wagon ever built, combining good styling with excellent load-carrying capacity. This fine example has been owned by Larry Myers, from Edmond, Oklahoma, for over 22 years

Left

A slight difference to the engine compartment than when originally built in 1955. Larry Myers installed a 350 ci small block in his Nomad, fitting it with a Sig Erson cam, Holley 750 cfm carburettor on a Weiand manifold and 205 fuel injected cylinder heads. A liberal sprinkling of chrome and the block colour keyed to the bodywork make a neat package. The engine is backed by a 350 Turbo Hydramatic transmission

Overleaf

The front end of the Nomad is standard '55 Chevy with extra stainless steel trim over the headlight peaks, but from the cowl back there are no common panels. Myers' Nomad is immaculate from every angle

136 bhp of the latest version of the 235 cubic inch Blue Flame six-cylinder inline engine, which was also available throughout the new range.

Behind the engine, customers could specify either a three-speed manual transmission, without or with overdrive, or a two-speed Powerglide automatic. Rear axle ratios with these transmissions were 3.70:1, 4.11:1 and 3.55:1 respectively.

Above
The interior of the Nomad is trimmed in Coral and Gray in a waffle pattern to the original specification. The upholstery colours provide a perfect match for the Coral and Shadow Grey two-tone paintwork

Right
The Nomad has many unique features, foremost among them being the pillarless hard top styling with one long expanse of glass behind the B pillar. The tailgate/liftgate assembly slopes at a much shallower angle than the standard wagon and is set off by the vertical trim strips on the tailgate. The full diameter rear fender cutouts looks as though they might have been created by a drag racer intent on stuffing some big slicks under the car, but they came that way from the factory. Larry Myers filled them with Cragar wheels carrying Michelin rubber. Note the Bel Air script on the rear fender – all Nomads came with the former's level of trim

Cheapest models were the One-Fifty series, 'plain Janes' in every sense. Available as two and four-door sedans, a two-door utility sedan and a two-door wagon, they had virtually no exterior brightwork, other than the bumpers, grille, light surrounds and door handles. Interiors were spartan, but practical. The utility sedan was interesting, being a normal sedan with a raised rear floor in place of the rear seat.

The Two-Tens offered a bit more style for a bit more money. They had stainless steel steel surrounds to the windshield and back window and along the beltline. A horizontal 'spear' ran along the rear fender to a point just behind the door and was linked to a vertical trim that ran down from the beltline dip (except on the wagons which did not have the dip; on these, the vertical trim ended about halfway between the horizontal trim and the beltline). They carried the same Chevrolet script

Above
Here's a fine example of a Bel Air sport coupe. Chrome wires set off the bright red paintwork beautifully, but at one time it looks as though the car sported two-tone paintwork – notice the rear fender trim

Right
Yes indeed, can't argue with that statement. Continental spare wheel carrier was an optional extra on all classic Chevies and provided more room in the trunk as well as a little extra class

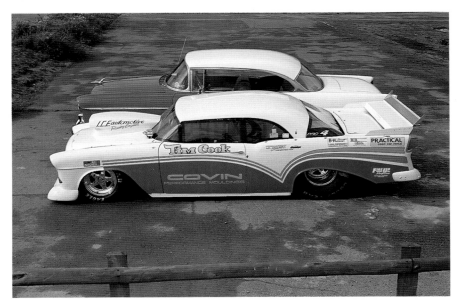

on the front fender as the One-Fifty versions. The interiors were better appointed and featured such niceties as armrests, a cigarette lighter and an ashtray.

Initially, the Two-Ten series comprised two- and four-door sedans, a Delray club coupe (a two-door sedan with a snazzy interior) and two- and four-door wagons, but half-way through 1955 a hard top sport coupe was added. This was effectively the same as the Bel Air sport coupe, but with Two-Ten trim.

Above
English drag racer Tim Cook has long had a love affair with classic Chevies, both on the street and on the strip, so it was natural that when he was looking to build a new car to contest the Pro-Modified class he should consider one of his favourites – a '55 sport coupe. This one, though, is all glassfibre and highly modified to boot, as you can see from the standard Bel Air next to it. The racer's body is shorter, narrower and lower than the standard car, and it sits on a purpose-built chrome-moly tube chassis, which rolls on Weld wheels and Goodyear tyres.

Left
The 540 ci Chevy iron block engine puts out a whopping 1050 bhp and is backed by a four-speed Lenco transmission. In his first season with the car, Tim set a new UK Pro-Modified record for the quarter mile of 7.69 seconds at 178 mph

At the top of the range were the Bel Airs: two- and four-door sedans, the sport coupe, a convertible and a four-door wagon. This line up was extended early in 1955 by the introduction of the attractive two-door Nomad wagon, which combined the usefulness of a wagon with the hard top styling of the coupe. The Bel Airs really stood out from the rest of the crowd, having extra stainless steel side trims on the front fenders and around the side windows which, together with the full wheel trims, made for plenty of glitter. Their appearance could be enhanced even further by the option of two-tone paintwork. Two styles were offered: one saw just the roof finished in a contrasting colour to the rest of the car, while the other had the roof, the trunk lid and rear panel and the upper portions of the rear fenders in that second colour.

Above
All the lightweight glassfibre body panels of Tim Cook's racer can be removed to provide easy access to any part of the car's chassis. The bodywork was carried out by his own company, Covin Performance Mouldings

Left
This shot shows just how much lower the racer is than a stock Bel Air sport coupe. Such radical modification was necessary to cut down on the built-in wind resistance of the standard body. While many other racers choose far more modern, 'slippery' designs, it is good to see the classic Chevy shape still up there with the winners on the quarter mile

To match the exterior, interiors were better appointed with carpeting rather than rubber mats and a choice of materials for upholstery. The coupe had a vinyl headliner with chrome trims. Press and public alike took to the new Chevy, praising its styling and performance. That performance was soon to be put to the test on the race track, where the car began making a mark for itself in a variety of different events, and it continues to do so to this day. Chevy had successfully thrown off its old staid image, something that was particularly apparent by its advertising, which leant heavily on the car's competition successes. One such ad shouted: 'Don't argue with this baby!' Indeed, the opposition had little with which to argue.

Above
At first glance, you might think that this two-tone grey sport coupe was just another nice, restored '55, but look again. See the 'bug catcher' peeking through the hood? Yes, this one sports a supercharger. The car is a curious combination of street machine (the blower and wheels), custom (hood shaved of 'bird' etc) and restoration (optional bumper guards), but what the heck, to each his own!

Right
Now that's what you call a clean engine compartment. Bright red paint, milled and polished aluminium and chrome plate add some real sparkle to this '55

Above
Merle Berg is a professional customiser and bodyman, and this Bel Air sport coupe is a prime example of his workmanship. He bought it in 1962, and it was only the second car he had ever owned. Between then and 1969, he carried out the major body modifications you see here; then he put the car in storage, only bringing it out again in 1986. Although the front and rear ends of the car have been heavily modified, it is still recognisably a '55 Chevy. The car sits four inches lower all round, thanks to lowering blocks at the rear and cut coils at the front, and it rolls on '56 Cadillac Eldorado wheels

Right
The front end of Merle's machine has been changed radically, the headlight surrounds having been pulled forwards and then flowed downwards into the lower pan. Chrome tube outlines the grille area with its unique centrepiece. All trim has been removed from the hood, too

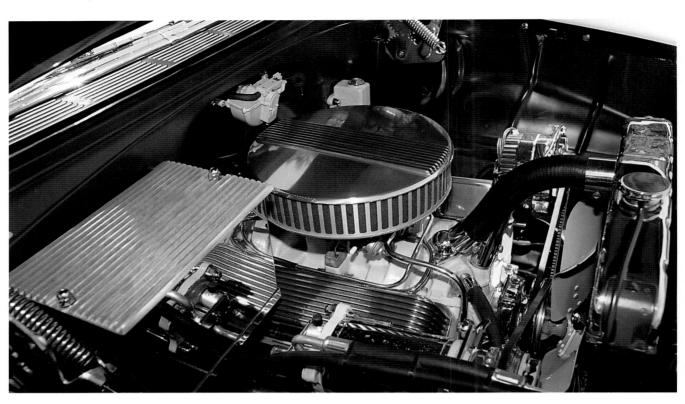

Above

At the rear, the familar lights have gone and the fenders extended to flow downwards into the rolled rear pan. Simple round rear lights are tunnelled into the pan, and the licence plate carries a simple message. While many purists might bemoan the fate of this particular Chevy, there is no doubting the quality of the workmanship that has gone into it, and it is a clear indication of the appeal of classic Chevies across a wide spectrum of automotive enthusiasts

Above left

This shot of Merle Berg's Chevy shows just how spacious the engine compartment is, making working on the engine a snap. This one's a stock 283 equipped with a four barrel carb and a set of Hooker headers

Left

The front seats are stock items, re-upholstered in silver Naugahyde, while the steering wheel came from a '59 Oldsmobile. The tarp over the back seat disguises the fact that at the time these photographs were taken the interior was unfinished. The upholstery provides a stark contrast to the exterior, which is finished in black primer

Above

The first Bel Air appeared in 1950 when Chevy introduced its hard top model, and the name was to be carried by the company's products through to 1959. But it's the classic models of 1955-57 that are remembered for popularising the name

Above right

Classic Chevies have always been popular with drag racers. Prior to racing this glassfibre-bodied, scaled-down '55 lookalike, Charles Carpenter used to race a steel-bodied sport coupe that laid claim to the title 'World's Fastest '55 Chevy'

Right

Thirty-five years after it was built, this Two-Ten two-door sedan is still a crowd pleaser at the drag strip. It's difficult to imagine a drag racing event without at least one classic Chevy in attendance

Above

Derald and Nola DeVries own this pristine example of a restored Bel Air two-door sedan. Sitting in the Oklahoma sun, it displays the clean lines of the 1955 model and demonstrates the effectiveness of the two-tone paint scheme. The licence plate 'SEBES 55' is in memory of Nola's grandfather, whose name was Sebe

Right

Pristine or what? The DeVries' sedan now sports a 283 ci small block rather than the original 265, but otherwise it looks just like it did when it rolled out of the factory. The engine is backed by a Powerglide transmission and stock running gear

Above

Thirty-five-years old and looking as good as new. The DeVries' two-door was brought back to its former glory by Sweetwood Restoration, who obviously know their job. The car originally came from Florida and had been ordered without a heater — not quite so good in its new home in Illinois!

Left

The beautiful interior of the sedan looks as though it's never been used. A non-stock accessory panel (just visible behind the steering wheel) carries three gauges to provide additional information about the engine's condition

Above

This is how the Two-Ten two-door looked when new. Notice the reduced amount of brightwork when compared to the Bel Air

Left

There once was a time when a high-riding Chevy street machine was considered a class act, and this Two-Ten two-door sedan evokes that period. Nowadays, however, most ride much closer to the pavement

Above

There is no mistaking that Philip Moules' sport coupe is a street machine with a vengeance. The bright red and white hard top was imported into England by Mick Howard, who became rather disillusioned with it after it fell off the jack one day, broke his leg and rolled down hill to demolish the rear wing of a BMW! Philip then bought the car from him and drove it for a while before completely stripping and rebuilding it to the high standard you see here

Right

The interior was retrimmed in black velour and vinyl before the car was imported from California

Above

The Chevy now packs a punch courtesy of a 360 ci AMC V8 equipped with a GMC 6:71 supercharger and backed by a Torqueflite transmission. This passes the power to the stock Chevy rear axle, which is controlled by adjustable gas shocks and a set of homemade ladder bars. The car rolls on Cragar wheels and Firestone tyres all round

Left

In pure street machine tradition, the front bumper has been removed to help weight transfer to the rear wheels; the inner fender panels have also been stripped out. Philip rebuilt the car completely himself, with help from his fiance Caroline and a couple of friends, doing the work in a garage that was actually shorter than the car! It's certainly a job he can be proud of

Above

Today, most classic Chevies are cherished by their owners and are often in better condition than when they came off the production line. This Two-Ten sedan is in excellent shape, and the licence plate gives some idea of the owner's obsession in keeping it that way

Above

Lance Denton's Bel Air convertible is a truly desirable car in immaculate condition. Note the accessory trims at the rear of the front fender openings, along the sill and at the tips of the rear bumper. The V-shaped crests below the rear lights indicate that the car is a V8 model, as opposed to a six-cylinder version

Above
The racer's stance comes from lowered suspension and a combination of Goodyear slicks and Mickey Thompson radials on Centerline wheels (3.5 inch at the front; 12 inch at the rear). To accommodate the massive slicks, the rear fender openings have been radiused

Right
Duncan Purssell's Two-Ten has had a long career as a racer, including a period during the sixties when it was regularly raced (illegally) on Van Nuys Boulevard in Los Angeles. Now the Fiat blue two-door resides in Essex, England, and is regularly campaigned on the drag strip. Under the one-piece glassfibre front end sits a 396 ci V8 equipped with an Erson .625 inch lift cam, smallpot, open chamber heads and a Holley 850 DD carburettor. The engine is backed by a Turbo 300 transmission which passes the power to a 9 inch Ford rear axle fitted with Strange shafts

1956: Hotter still

As 1955 rolled to a close, it was clear that despite the enormous success of the new Chevy, the company would have to offer something new (or at least something that looked new) if they were to hold their own in the very competitive US automotive market. A completely new car would be out of the question on grounds of cost, besides which they had a very good package which had not been exploited to the full. Thus, a facelift was the answer, together with a few mechanical improvements.

The front and rear ends of the car were completely restyled, although the central portion of the body remained the same. At the front, the fenders were lengthened slightly and had more pronounced peaks over the headlights, while the hood was also lengthened to match.

One of the most obvious changes was the grille. Chevy had bowed to public pressure and had dispensed with the neat 'egg crate' of the '55 model. In its place was a full-width chrome lattice incorporating rectangular parking lights at each end, the chrome trim wrapping round the front of the fender, above the bumper, to the wheel opening. The grille was formed in a shallow V shape, and was matched by the bumper and hood lip.

The sides of the front fenders were also slightly flatter than the earlier versions, and the whole effect was to give the front end a much 'sharper' appearance.

The rear fenders also came in for restyling, the wheel openings being made teardrop shaped, and the upper rear corners being formed into embryonic fins. These, together with the lengthened lower portions of the fenders, gave a V-shaped profile when looked at side on. Overall, the changes combined to give the car a longer, lower look.

The simple, neat rear lights of the '55 gave way to larger chromed housings, each containing a small round tail light, a small round reflector and a reversing light. The unit on the left-hand side of the car was hinged and opened to reveal the fuel filler cap tucked inside the fender.

Right
Nineteen-fifty-six saw new front and rear end treatments, and while the grille still retained a semblance of its original 'egg crate' style, it was stretched in width and incorporated side lights at its extremities. The headlights were surrounded by more pronounced peaks, and a shallow V-shaped trim appeared below the company crest on V8 engined cars

Above

Gary French's Bel Air sport coupe is a tidy example of the breed and clearly shows the change in profile compared to the '55 model. Front and rear fenders were new, although the roof, doors and centre of the body were the same as before. Note the stainless steel side trim that carries the two-tone treatment right through to the front fender

Above right

The Two-Ten had simpler side trims, a single spear running from the front fender, through the door and sweeping down across the rear fender. It was joined to the beltline dip by a short vertical trim. The two-tone paint scheme is totally different to that used on the Bel Air models, the roof and sides below the trim being in a colour that contrasts with that of the upper sides, the trunk lid and hood. Note the small trim running between the spear and the front fender opening to separate the two colours

Right

All the models of classic Chevy have provided the raw material for street machines, and this Bel Air sedan is no exception. Bright yellow paint, raised rear suspension, traction bars and those carburettors peeking through the hood leave you in no doubt that this car means business

Above
Don and Pat Wheeler, from Aurora, Missouri, are real classic Chevy enthusiasts; in addition to this superb example of a '56 Bel Air sport coupe, they also own a '55 Bel Air convertible and a '57 Bel Air sport coupe

Right
The Wheelers' hard top features many of the optional accessories that were offered when the car was built. Those wire wheel covers, whitewall tyres and the deluxe bumper guards are among them. They show how Chevy was shaking off its reputation for building staid, family cars

JUL MO
56-CHEV
·HISTORIC VEHICLE·

Mechanically, Chevrolet made changes to the suspension to improve the car's handling, lengthening the front springs and reducing their poundage, and fitting larger bushes to the rear springs.

Alterations to the V8 engine option made 'The Hot One' even hotter. The 265 cubic inch engine was still available with the three-speed manual transmission (with or without overdrive) or Powerglide automatic. When packaged with the latter, it came with a higher-lift camshaft that raised bhp to 170 at 4400 rpm. However, an optional power pack comprising a four-barrel carburettor and suitable inlet manifold, higher compression heads, a high-lift cam and dual exhausts pushed that figure to 205 bhp at 4600 rpm. Even more power could be squeezed from it with a dual four-barrel set up used on the Corvette: 225 bhp at 5200 rpm.

Above
Finished in a two-tone scheme of Nassau blue and Harbor blue, this Bel Air is a prime example of the type. Cherished by its owners, the car only clocks up about 1000 miles a year

Left
The optional continental spare wheel kit provided more room in the trunk and gave the car even more style. Note the different tail lights compared to the '55 with greater emphasis on brightwork. Note, too, the exhaust tips below the bumper

Improvements were also made to the engine's lubrication system, to the electrical system and to the carburettor air filter, reducing induction noise.

The 235 cubic inch 'Blue Flame' six also came in for alteration, being fitted with a higher lift cam, hydraulic lifters and higher-compression head to raise bhp to 140 at 4200 rpm. All the models in the range could be specified with either this engine or the V8, the latter cars being distinguished by large V-shaped emblems on hood and trunk lid.

As before, there were One-Fifty, Two-Ten and Bel Air series, although the total number of models was increased and there was a general improvement in specification across the range.

The One-Fifty series comprised the same four models as before, but was a little less basic with jazzier interior trim incorporating gold-flecked upholstery. Outside, they were provided with a stainless steel side trim

Above
The Wheelers have every right to be proud of their sport coupe – it's period perfect

Left
Like it's just rolled out of the showroom. The interior is perfect and original. The 'bowtie' perforations in the dashboard trim were dropped for the '56 model in favour of simple slots, and this car is fitted with the optional factory air conditioning and a Wonder Bar radio

that ran back from just behind the headlight to meet a second trim that extended downwards from the beltline dip. This made it possible to offer a two-tone paint scheme on any of these cars. Extra brightwork was also used to enhance the front and rear screen surrounds.

The number of Two-Ten models was increased from six to eight by the addition of a sport sedan (a four-door version of the sport coupe) and a nine-passenger, four-door Beauville wagon. Exterior trim on the Two-Tens comprised a stainless steel 'spear' that ran back from just behind the headlight, across the door and down across the rear fender to the rear bumper in a gentle curve, being met by a sloping trim that descended from the beltline dip. The addition of a small trim piece between the 'spear' and the top of the front fender opening allowed two-tone paint treatments, whereby the roof and lower portion of the body were painted in one colour and the upper body portion in another.

Above
You have to look twice to notice the custom tricks applied to this Two-Ten two-door sedan. The bright red paint is set off by the Centerline wheels and the white upholstery, while the tube grille and a dechromed hood provide the finishing touches

Left
In place of the 'bird', a shallow arrowhead has been formed to blend in with the surface of the hood, while the licence plate says it all

As before, the Bel Airs were the top of the range, the same body styles as 1955 being available with the addition of a four-door sport sedan. The interiors of these cars were upholstered in a V-shaped theme with a combination of nylon-faced cloth and leather-grained vinyl, set off by thick carpet on the floor. They featured extra side trims, compared to the Two-Ten, that allowed a 'spear' of contrasting colour to run right through the side of the car to just behind the headlight.

Compared to some of its competitors (and indeed the following year's Chevy), the restyled 1956 model was quite restrained in appearance and, once again, received praise from press and public alike. The performance, handling and appearance of the car were all welcomed, and in common with its predecessor, it did as well on the track as on the road. It kept Chevrolet ahead of Ford that year, despite a general drop in sales throughout the industry, but to keep that lead, yet another restyle was called for as 1957 came into view.

Above
James Smith owns this Two-Ten four-door sedan. It's so well looked after that it looks brand new

Left
An unusual colour combination makes this Bel Air convertible stand out from the crowd. Note the fender skirts and spotlight

Above

Before Tim Cook built and began racing his glassfibre '55 Chevy (see page 69), he campaigned this glassfibre replica of a chopped '56 Bel Air sport coupe. Originally, it had been intended to build a racer based on an original, steel-bodied car, but the car he bought was in such a poor state that this simply was not feasible. Fortunately, Tim is in the glassfibre business and his company, Covin Performance Mouldings was able to produce the body you see here

Right

Power for the racer comes from a 572 ci V8 based on an aluminium Donovan block with Dart heads, a BRC crank, Carillo rods and Manley pistons. The cam is a Reed roller item and the ignition MSD. A pair of Holley 1050 Dominator carburettors sits atop a homemade manifold. This setup produces 800 bhp, although considerably more power is available if the engine is fed a dose of nitrous oxide. Backing the engine is a McLeod twin-disc clutch and a four-speed Lenco transmission

Above

The full-size glassfibre body sits on a custom-built tubular chassis, which rolls on Weld wheels with Goodyear rubber at the front and Mickey Thompson slicks at the rear

Left

The purposeful interior of Tim Cook's glassfibre racer features a full roll cage and anodised aluminium panelling. Note the shift levers for the Lenco transmission

Above
Sedan deliveries are a relatively rare sight; Gene Ward's example is super clean, and a superb advertisement for his business. Based on a two-door wagon bodyshell, the sedan delivery came with One-Fifty trim — note the single stainless steel side spear

Right
The full-width grille of the facelifted '56 model made the car look wider, although it was not. This Bel Air sport coupe clearly illustrates the phenomenon

Above
Only the wheels and traction bars give a hint that there might be more to this Bel Air sport coupe than meets the eye

Above left
Just as classic Chevies have always been used for building street machines, many have also received both mild and radical custom modifications. Jim Wagner's Bel Air sport coupe is a prime example of the mild custom and sports many of the features that would have been seen on similar cars in the early sixties, such as a tube grille, chrome reversed wheels, Appleton spotlights and lakes pipes. The whole package is neatly set off by hot pink flames

Left
Once again, the Nomad was best looking of the wagons and carried over the hard top styling from the '55 model. Unlike that model, however, its rear fender cut-outs matched those of the sedans and coupes. The side trim delineating the two-tone paintwork was different, though, the vertical portion being formed to follow the line of the roof pillar, whereas on the other models it sloped in the opposite direction. Uniquely, the Nomad also carried chrome V-shaped emblems beneath the rear lights of V8-engined cars, while other models that year had a large 'V' on the trunk lid or tailgate

Right

Kirby and Pat Lawrence, of Cottage Grove, Minnesota, own this beautiful mild custom Bel Air sport coupe. Unlike some customs that go over the top, this one is extremely tasteful. In fact, it is a copy of Kirby's first ever '56 Chevy, which he bought new in 1956 and customised in 1958. One striking feature is the custom-made tube grille, which is emphasised by the filled and louvred hood

Above

When Kirby and Pat found the hard top in southern Minnesota it was a non-runner and had been towed there from California. Now the bright Porsche Indian red coupe receives its motive power from a 327 ci V8, which is a good step forwards from the old 265 lump that would have inhabited the engine compartment. The beautiful exterior finish is carried over to the engine bay, which is spotless

Above
To match the hood, the trunk lid of Kirby's coupe has been filled and now only carries the licence plate. The aerial has been frenched into the top of the rear fender. All in all, the car is very impressive and warrants careful study to appreciate the visual impact of the modifications

Left
The tail lights of the '56 appear considerably more complex than those of the '55 models, the lens area being smaller and the brightwork larger. Kirby added blue dot-lenses to his rear lights to give that purple glow so popular when cruising at night

Above
Kirby's customised Chevy has definitely got a 'serious attitude' … The front suspension of Kirby's '56 was lowered to get that nose-down stance, while the rear was left stock. Side spears from a Two-Ten were used in place of the more complex Bel Air items and blend in well with the simple look of the car, while chrome reversed wheels with baby moon hubcaps and wide whitewall tyres complete the look

Above right
Kirby had local upholsterer Jeff Erichson retrim the interior in silver grey rolled and pleated velour with red piping, added a '58 Impala steering wheel, then filled and louvred the dashboard before it was painted to match the exterior

Right
The entire car is absolutely pristine, as can be seen from the trunk

Above

Those '59 Cadillac tail light lenses have always been popular with customisers, probably from the day they first appeared. This Bel Air convertible not only sports two such lenses on each side, but has had its tail light assemblies sunk into the rear fenders as well

Right

All the classic Chevies provide plenty of room under the hood for the engine, which is great when you need to do any work. It also means that you can drop in extra goodies, like this B&M supercharger, without it being too obvious from the outside

Above

Karl Kuhnke is a dealer in classic American cars in England, and typical of the sort of car he trades in is this completely restored Bel Air convertible. Even in rainswept England, the soft-top cruiser is a desirable car

Left

Finished in Sienna gold and Adobe beige, the convertible was restored to original condition in Ohio about six years ago and recently imported into England where, by now, it will be giving some lucky new owner many pleasurable miles

Above
The convertible features several desirable factory options, including a Power Pak (four-barrel carburettor and twin exhausts), a continental spare wheel kit and a radio

Right
The interior was completely retrimmed when the car was restored and matches the paint scheme

Above

Here's a Two-Ten two-door that certainly does bear closer inspection. Marty Vanderhoff's bright orange example has full two-tone side trim (note the small vertical trim between the spear and front fender opening) and presumably came from the factory that way. Lowered suspension and glittering wheels make for a class act that's difficult to follow

Above right

A snip at $5500? Two-Ten two-door sedan now has a V8 in place of the original six and a four-speed manual transmission. It may be a bargain, but then again ... Only close inspection by an expert will reveal the condition and true value of the car

Right

Compared to the '55, the '56 model's tail lights seem to have a much smaller lens area, although the lights are still very effective. Left-hand light unit conceals the fuel filler cap and is hinged to provide access

1957: The engineer's dream

As 1957 opened, Chevrolet faced particularly strong competition from Ford and Chrysler, both of whom had launched new designs. Chevrolet, however, had to make do with a third facelift of the original 1955 model, and while it was far more radical in appearance than the '56, it was still a two-year-old design under the skin. Its saving grace was a new version of the V8 engine, boasting 283 cubic inches and available with Rochester 'Ramjet' fuel injection to boost bhp to 283 – one bhp per cubic inch: 'the engineer's dream', as Chevy put it in one of their ads. There were other mechanical changes, too, although not all were improvements over the earlier models.

In terms of its outward appearance, the '57 certainly was a 'sharp' looking car, with a major reworking of the front end treatment together with a substantial change to the rear end of the body. As in 1956, however, the central portion of the shell, including the doors and roof, remained unchanged. This had one slight advantage compared to the opposition who were going for lower rooflines: the Chevy had more headroom inside – something appreciated by taller drivers and inveterate hat wearers!

A longer, lower hood line was matched by longer front fenders with distinctive peaks over the headlights. The lower hood line had been made possible by the removal of the interior fresh air intakes at the base of the windshield. These had been replaced by ducts that ran from grilles set above the headlights, through the fenders to the firewall. The hood also had a pair of 'wind splits' set near the leading edge in place of the single 'bird' of the earlier models.

Right
Nineteen-fifty-seven saw some dramatic restyling of the classic Chevy, both at front and rear, although as in the previous year, the central section of the car remained virtually unchanged. Among the most striking features is the front bumper which sweeps upwards at the ends to join the front fenders and meet the chrome trim that provides a lip to the hood. Both bumper and trim form a surround for the slotted grille with its central 'floating' bar and side lights. Headlamp surrounds have even more pronounced peaks and incorporate air intakes to feed the car's interior, while the hood features a pair of 'wind splits'

Above

The sweeping lines of the '57 Bel Air lend themselves to the convertible design. Note the gold louvre trims on the front fenders, the brushed aluminium insert on the rear fender and the gold rear fender script – all standard features on the Bel Air

Left

One of the nicest Bel Air convertibles you're ever likely to see belongs to Phil and Sallie Miller from Little Rock, Arkansas. The car was restored to original condition over a period of 18 months and has been owned by the Millers for about five years

The front end facelift was completed by a heavy-looking combined bumper and full-width concave mesh grille with a central 'floating' bar that carried a parking light at each end. This was quite unlike anything seen on the previous years' models and was the car's most striking feature.

At the rear, the fenders had been formed into true fins at their ends, giving the side profile a swept-back appearance. Light units were positioned near the base of the fender, just above the bumper. The latter had oval openings just below the lights which, originally, had been intended as exits for the exhaust pipes. However, due to fears about the exhaust staining the surrounding brightwork, this idea was dropped and the openings closed off, or filled with a pair of reversing lights.

The really hot news, however, was the 283 cubic inch version of the V8. The extra capacity came from increasing the bore to 3.875 inches.

Above
Whereas both '55 and '56 hoods feature central 'birds', the '57 has a pair of 'wind splits' set into the hood's top surface. Those on the Miller's car are simply perfect

Right
Spotless engine compartment of Phil Miller's convertible belies the fact that the car covers some 6000 miles each year, visiting classic Chevy events across the US. The engine is a 283 with Powerglide transmission

This engine could be had with a two-barrel carburettor, single four-barrel, dual four-barrels or the 'Ramjet' fuel injection; compression ratios ranged from 8.5:1 to 10.5:1; and higher lift cams were available.

Improvements were also made to the inlet and exhaust passages to improve volumetric efficiency; to the ignition with longer-reach spark plugs, heat shields for the plug leads and a new distributor; and to the

Above
The interior was restored to original condition by Dowen Upholstery and complements the Matador red exterior paintwork

Right
Stock wheel trims are set off by whitewall tyres

Above
There is no doubt that the '57 model is the most elegant of the classic Chevy convertibles, and the Miller's is a superb example of the breed

Left
Great changes were made to the tail lights for the '57 model, as revealed by Phil Miller's car. Because of the extended fin design, the light units were moved to the base of the fender, just above the rear bumper, which contained reversing lights. Originally, the exhausts were to have terminated at the reversing light positions in the bumper, but this idea was eventually dropped because of the inevitable discolouration that would have occurred

front and intermediate main bearings, which were thicker. The result was that the 283 offered outputs ranging from 185 bhp at 4600 rpm to 283 bhp at 6200 rpm.

In addition to the 283 cubic inch engine, the original 265 cubic inch V8 was still available, as was the 235 cubic inch six. The former came with the three-speed manual transmission (with or without overdrive), as did the six, which could also be specified with the two-speed Powerglide. The 283 came with a choice of Powerglide or Turboglide automatic or three-speed manual with options of overdrive and close ratios. Rear axle ratios were 3.36:1, 3.55:1 and 4.11:1 for automatic, manual and overdrive transmissions respectively.

The chassis was strengthened with a new front crossmember, and improvements were made to the brakes and to the suspension to improve roadholding. However, not all the press testers of the day agreed with this, preferring the tauter handling of the '56 to the softer ride of the '57. Another change in this area was from 15 inch diameter

Above
Here's a clean example of a rare Two-Ten sport coupe, distinguishable from the Bel Air by the painted panel between the stainless trim on the rear fender and the Chevrolet script on that panel. Bel Airs also had such items as the hood script and 'V' (on V8 models), trims on the front fender louvres and the Bel Air script in gold anodised aluminium, no less. These items, plus the fairly radical nature of the restyling exercise, tend to make the Bel Airs look a little gaudy, particularly to European eyes

wheels to 14 inch diameter versions with lower-pressure tyres. If nothing else, these helped lower the car a little more.

Once again, Chevy offered One-Fifty, Two-Ten and Bel Air series of the new car, all three being available in the same models as before with the exception that the nine-passenger Bel Air Beauville wagon was replaced by a six-passenger Townsman version.

The One-Fifty series had a simple horizontal side 'spear' running along the rear fender and on to the door with a second trim running down to it from the beltline dip (much like the '55 Two-Ten trim). Both Two-Ten and Bel Air, however, had a stainless steel trim that ran back from just behind the headlight and curved down to meet the rear bumper, while a second horizontal trim ran across the rear fender to meet the first trim ahead of the rear wheel. These two trims created a triangular area on the rear fender which could be painted a different colour on two-tone Two-Tens or contain a brushed aluminium panel on Bel Airs. These had the further distinction of having various emblems

Below
This pretty Two-Ten sedan has received the mild custom treatment with lowered suspension, a louvred hood and scalloped paint. The classic Chevy series is probably the most versatile when it comes to modification

and the grille mesh in gold anodised aluminium. They also had full diameter wheel trims as standard.

The interior of the cars also came in for improvement, the dashboard being redesigned to make the instruments more visible.

As before, the Chevy put up some superb track performances, particularly with the new, more powerful 283 cubic inch. V8, but it was during this time that Chevrolet – together with several other manufacturers – decided to pull out of direct involvement in racing. That did not stop the Chevy being raced of course, but Chevrolet were not

Left
'Capable of leaping tall trees with one mighty bound' ... well, almost. Jerry Asleck's four-door Bel Air wagon looks set for some serious cross-country action. Jerry installed the running gear and half the chassis from a 4 ¥ 4 Chevy truck beneath his six-passenger Townsman wagon, added maroon paint and tinted glass, not to mention Michelin XC All Terrain tyres, and came up with with this stunning package

Below
Roy and Sandy Buntin from Moore, Oklahoma, own this bright blue Bel Air sport coupe, which has been on the receiving end of a few changes since it left the factory in 1957. Roy and son Paul applied the blue paint and set it off with a sparkling set of TruSpoke wire wheels, while the matching blue upholstery was sewn by Sandy

in a position to take advantage of its successes. No longer would owners of the opposition's cars be urged not to 'argue with this baby!'

Despite the car's many good points, Chevrolet did not fare well against Ford that year it was time for a change again, and the company had a new car waiting in the wings. However, never again would the company produce a series of cars that had the appeal of the '55-'57 models. In subsequent years, their cars became bigger, heavier and more sluggish. None is pursued as doggedly by the enthusiast and collector as that trio from the fifties. None still offers such appeal to youth and the young at heart.

Above
Sandy extended her upholstery skills to the trunk, making up panels to line the sides and a cover for the spare tyre. Upholstered inserts have even been added to the underside of the trunk lid

Left
The glittering engine compartment of the Buntin's hardtop now sports a 350 ci small block in place of the original 283, and this is topped by a pair of Carter AFB carburettors. Liberal use of braided hose, as well as chrome and polished aluminium ensures that plenty of elbow grease is needed to keep it looking spotless

Above
Here's a superb example of a stock Bel Air sedan, which belongs to Floyd Ploesser.
The pink and white four-door is as straight as a die

Right
Although most classic Chevies you see tend to have V8 engines, Floyd Ploesser's Bel Air
has its original 'Blue Flame' 235 ci six, which was good for 125 bhp at 4000 rpm. The
'Blue Flame' was a good reliable engine, and in the spacious engine compartment of
any of the classic Chevies was easy to work on

Above
Finished in Ford Signal yellow, Terry Calder's wagon/delivery rolls on TruSpoke wire wheels wrapped with 205/70 VR 15 rubber. The car was rebuilt to essentially stock specification and is fitted with a 283 V8 and two-speed Powerglide transmission

Above left
Terry Calder's Two-Ten wagon is one of a kind, having been converted at some stage in its life to a partial sedan delivery. This work was performed while the car was still in the States, but now the bright yellow four-door lives in England, where Terry found it after setting out to look for 'something different'. Unfortunately, Terry's find proved to be less of a bargain than he thought, as it very quickly managed to dump all the oil from the engine, gearbox and back axle. There followed some 14 months of rebuilding, during which everything on the car was renovated or renewed. The result you see was obviously worth all that dedication

Left
The rear side windows of the wagon have been panelled in, much like those of a delivery, and the area behind the rear seat has been neatly carpeted. The liftgate now sports a smaller window than it had originally

Above

Now and again, classic Chevy hunters come across real treasure. Take this One-Fifty Handyman wagon, for example. In 33 years, it had had one little old lady owner and covered only 96,000 miles. It was completely original right down to the paint. The One-Fifty models were the most basic and came with few frills. Note the simple trim on the rear fender

Above
Out to make a good impression on the judges at the Classic Chevy Convention in Oklahoma City, Doug Kain gives his two-door Two-Ten sedan a thorough going over after his trip up from Texas. Note how the trim on the top of the rear fenders stops about a third of the way along, whereas on the Bel Air it continues to the base of the rear window

Above

B J Bucher's two-door sedan began life as a Two-Ten, but now sports bits of trim from various models. The low, black hot rod also has a Jaguar independent rear end and a 350 ci small block V8 in place of the original 265

Right

Rochester fuel injection was available as an option on the 283 ci V8 in 1957, although few buyers took it up and there were a few teething troubles with the early examples. Now well and truly sorted, this glittering setup in Bucher's sedan works just fine

Above
Another unique classic Chevy wagon is this shortened Bel Air, which carries a Nomad script on the tailgate and the licence plate 'HALF MAD'. It certainly makes you stop and look twice – and you can't see the join!

Left
Rear fender script leaves you in no doubt about the power source in this Two-Ten sedan

Above

This Bel Air sport coupe has received the custom treatment with turnpike cruiser skirts, Appleton spotlights, lakes pipes and a Corvette grille. Note the absence of door handles and hood 'wind splits'. The tail low stance of the car is also typical of many customs

Left

The intakes incorporated into the headlight surrounds on '57 models provide fresh air to the car's interior. This feature was criticised by some at the time who suggested that the intakes would allow exhaust fumes to reach the interior in slow moving traffic, or become caked with snow and'ice in severe winter weather. Neither appears to have happened

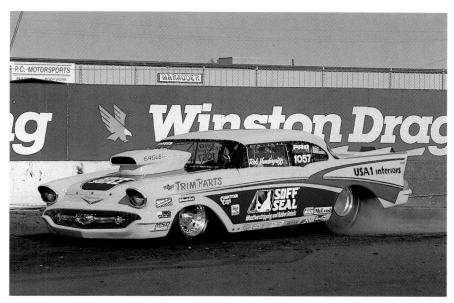

Above

Driven by Bob Vandergriff, this 7/8 scale sport coupe is capable of turning quarter-mile times in the seven second bracket and speeds of 200 mph. It is essentially a dragster with a body and features a full tubular chassis and big block Chevy engine

Left

Larry Fischer warms the tyres of his Bel Air sedan before another quick trip down the quarter mile

Above

Of all the classic Chevies, the Nomad models are among the most sought after, although surprisingly when they were introduced in the fifties they did not receive quite the same attention. Today, however, the sharp, hard top styling of the Nomad wagons generates considerable enthusiasm. This bright red '57 now lives in England, being owned by Ken Robbins, a died-in-the-wool classic Chevy fan of many years' standing. Before obtaining the Nomad, Ken had a '55 Bel Air sport coupe, and today he spends some of his spare time editing the Classic Journal for members of the Classic Chevy Club of Great Britain. It took five years for the Nomad to reach the condition you see here — five years well spent, obviously

Above right

The Nomad's interior has been spiced up with black pleated vinyl upholstery and a Grant woodrim steering wheel. The colum-mounted tachometer ensures that gearshifts are made at optimum rpm

Right
Nomads have much more style than the regular wagons and carry special badging

Above
The slope of the liftgate/tailgate emphasises the sharpness of the rear fender fins. With the exception of Fenton Ramrod wheels, the exterior of Ken Robbins' Nomad is completely stock

Right
Sitting in the engine compartment of Ken Robbins' Nomad is a 327 ci engine equipped with a high-performance cam and heads, a Holley Street Dominator inlet manifold and a Holley 600 cfm four-barrel carburettor. Exhaust gases are passed through custom-built headers to a pair of Turbo mufflers, while backing the engine is a four-speed Muncie gearbox

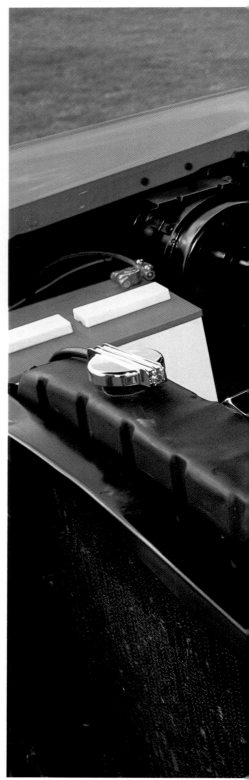

Above

When Michael Mattews goes drag racing, he goes in style. Not only does he race this clean Two-Ten sedan, but he tows it to and from the strip with the fine '55 Chevy pickup in the background. The two-door sedan enjoyed a long career as a racer in the US, under the name 'Thomas Flyer', before being imported into England. Michael bought it three years ago and, with the help of Gary Healy and Jeff Hauser, set about making it even more competitive

Right

A removable one-piece glassfibre front makes access to the 427 ci engine much simpler. Michael contemplates the coming action from the bed of his pickup, while Gary Healy (far right) and assistant do some fine tuning

Above

The rear portion of the sedan's chassis was built by Taylor Engineering, of Wittier, California. The rear suspension comprises ladder bars and Koni coil-over shocks, while Wilwood brakes provide stopping power. Finished in Cobalt blue with a blue pearl roof and fender flash, Michael Mattews' racer rolls on Goodyear rubber wrapped around Centerline wheels

Left

The engine itself features an Isky roller cam, open–chamber heads, an Edelbrock Victor Jnr inlet manifold, a Holley 850 cfm four-barrel carburettor and MSD electronic ignition. Custom exhaust headers were made up by Gary Healy's company, Gary's Shack. Behind the engine is a Turbo 400 transmission, equipped with an 8 inch converter and manual valve body, that passes the power to an Oldsmobile rear axle equipped with 4.88:1 gears. The full tubular front chassis, built by Jeff Hauser, features Strange Engineering struts and discs and a Pinto rack and pinion

Above
Old Chevies never die — they just get faster!

Above

Now why didn't they make them this way back in 1957? Gray Bradley's Nomad-based pickup sure is a super-looking truck

Specifications

1955 SPECIFICATIONS

Engine	Cu In	Comp ratio	Bore	Stroke	Gross HP	Net HP	Carburettor	Transmission
Blue Flame 123 – 6 cyl	235	7.5	3–9/16"	3–15/16"	123@ 3800 rpm	109 @ 3600 rpm	Single Barrel	3-Speed Overdrive Powerglide
Blue Flame 136 – 6 cyl	235	7.5	3–9/16"	3–15/16"	136 @ 4200 rpm	121 @ 3800 rpm	Single Barrel	3-Speed Overdrive Powerglide
Turbo-fire 8 cyl	265	8.0	3–3/4"	3"	162 @ 4400 rpm	137 @ 4000 rpm	2-Barrel	3-Speed Overdrive Powerglide
Turbo-Fire 8 cyl	265	8.0	3–3/4"	3"	180 @ 4600 rpm	160 @ 4200 rpm	4-Barrel	3-Speed Overdrive Powerglide

1955 DIMENSIONS

(Inches): Wheelbase 115; overall length 195.6 (station wagons 197.1); overall height 60.5 (hardtop/convertible 59.1, station wagons 60.8, Nomad 60.7); overall width 74; front tack 58; rear track 58.8; ground clearance 6.5.

1956 SPECIFICATIONS

Engine	Cu In	Comp ratio	Bore	Stroke	Gross HP	Net HP	Carburettor	Transmission
Blue-Flame 140 – 6 cyl	235	8.0	3–9/16"	3–15/16"	140 @ 4200 rpm	125 @ 4000 rpm	Single Barrel	3-Speed Overdrive Powerglide
Turbo-Fire 162 – 8 cyl	265	8.0	3–3/4"	3"	162 @ 4400 rpm	137 @ 4000 rpm	2-Barrel	3-Speed Overdrive Powerglide
Turbo-Fire 170 – 8 cyl	265	8.0	3–3/4"	3"	170 @ 4400 rpm	141 @ 4000 rpm	2-Barrel	3-Speed Overdrive Powerglide
Turbo-Fire 205 – 8 cyl	265	8.0	3–3/4"	3"	205 @ 4600 rpm	170 @ 4200 rpm	4-Barrel	3-Speed Overdrive Powerglide
Turbo-Fire 225 – 8 cyl	265	9.25	3–3/4"	3"	225 @ 5200 rpm	196 @ 4800 rpm	Dual 4-Barrel	3-Speed Overdrive Powerglide

1956 DIMENSIONS

(Inches): Wheelbase 115; overall length 197.5 (station wagons 200.8); overall height 60.5 (hardtop/convertible 59.1, station wagons 60.8, Nomad 60.7); overall width 74 (hardtops and convertible 72.9, station wagons 74); front tack 58; rear track 58.8; ground clearance 6.5.

1957 SPECIFICATIONS

Engine	Cu In	Comp ratio	Bore	Stroke	Gross HP	Net HP	Carburettor	Transmission
Blue Flame 140 – 6 cyl	235	8.0	3–9/16"	3–15/16"	140 @ 4200 rpm	125 @ 4000 rpm	Single Barrel	3-Speed Overdrive Powerglide
Turbo-Fire 265 – 8 cyl	265	8.0	3–3/4"	3"	162 @ 4400 rpm	137 @ 4000 rpm	2-Barrel	3-Speed Overdrive Powerglide
Turbo-Fire 283 – 8 cyl	283	8.5	3–7/8"	3"	185 @ 4600 rpm	150 @ 4600 rpm	2-Barrel	Powerglide Turboglide
Super Turbo-Fire 283 – 8 cyl	283	9.5	3–7/8"	3"	220 @ 4800 rpm	190 @ 4600 rpm	4-Barrel	3-Speed Overdrive Automatic transmission
8 cylinder	283	9.5	3–7/8"	3"	245 @ 5000 rpm	215 @ 4800 rpm	Dual 4-Barrel	3-Speed Close-Ratio Automatic transmission
8 cylinder	283	9.5	3–7/8"	3"	250 @ 5000 rpm	225 @ 4800 rpm	Fuel Injection	3-Speed Close-Ratio Automatic transmission
8 cylinder	283	9.5	3–7/8"	3"	270 @ 6000 rpm	230 @ 6000 rpm	Dual 4-Barrel	3-Speed Close-Ratio
8 cylinder	283	10.5	3–7/8"	3"	283 @ 6200 rpm	240 @ 5600 rpm	Fuel Injection	3-Speed Close-Ratio

1957 DIMENSIONS

(Inches): Wheelbase 115; overall length 200; overall height 59.9 (two-door hardtop 58.5, four-door hardtop and convertible 58.4, station wagons 60.1, Nomad 58.8); overall width 73.9; front tack 58; rear track 58.8; ground clearance 6.0.

1955 MODELS

Model no	Body style	Production	Weight (lbs)	Price ($)
One-Fifty				
1502	sedan, 2 dr	66,416	3080	1784
1503	sedan, 4 dr	29,898	3135	1827
1512	sedan, 2 dr utility	11,196	3055	1692
1529	Handyman wagon, 2 dr	17,936	3260	2129
Two-Ten				
2102	sedan, 2 dr	249,105	3115	1874
2103	sedan, 4 dr	317,724	3150	1918
2124	Delray club coupe	115,584	3115	1934
2154	sport coupe	11,675	3140	2058
2129	Handyman wagon, 2 dr	28,918	3300	2178
2109	Townsman wagon, 4 dr	82,303	3340	2226
Bel Air				
2402	sedan, 2 dr	168,313	3125	1987
2403	sedan, 4 dr	345,372	3170	2031
2454	sport coupe	185,562	3165	2166
2434	convertible	41,292	3285	2305
2429	Nomad wagon, 2 dr	8,530	3335	2571
2409	Beauville wagon, 4 dr	24,313	3355	2361

1956 MODELS

Model no	Body style	Production	Weight (lbs)	Price ($)
One-Fifty				
1502	sedan, 2 dr	82,384	3144	1925
1503	sedan, 4 dr	51,544	3186	1968
1512	sedan, 2 dr utility	9,879	3107	1833
1529	Handyman wagon, 2 dr	13,487	3289	2270
Two-Ten				
2102	sedan, 2 dr	205,545	3157	2011
2103	sedan, 4 dr	283,125	3192	2054
2124	Delray club coupe	56,382	3162	2070
2154	sport coupe	18,616	3184	2162
2113	sport sedan	20,021	3242	2216
2129	Handyman wagon, 2 dr	22,038	3324	2314
2109	Townsman wagon, 4 dr	113,656	3361	2362
2119	Beauville wagon, 4 dr	17,988	3480	2447

Model no	Body style	Production	Weight (lbs)	Price ($)
Bel Air				
2402	sedan, 2 dr	104,849	3177	2124
2403	sedan, 4 dr	269,798	3211	2167
2454	sport coupe	128,382	3212	2275
2413	sport sedan	103,602	3260	2329
2434	convertible	41,268	3320	2443
2429	Nomad wagon, 2 dr	8,103	3342	2707
2419	Beauville wagon, 4 dr	13,279	3496	2581

1957 MODELS

Model no	Body style	Production	Weight (lbs)	Price ($)
One-Fifty				
1502	sedan, 2 dr	70,774	3207	2096
1503	sedan, 4 dr	52,266	3232	2148
1512	sedan, 2 dr utility	8,300	3159	1985
1529	Handyman wagon, 2 dr	14,740	3402	3402
Two-Ten				
2102	sedan, 2 dr	162,090	3221	2222
2103	sedan, 4 dr	260,401	3266	2275
2124	Delray club coupe	25,644	3216	2262
2154	sport coupe	22,631	3256	2304
2113	sport sedan	16,178	3316	2370
2129	Handyman wagon, 2 dr	17,528	3402	2502
2109	Townsman wagon, 4 dr	127,803	3457	2556
2119	Beauville wagon, 4 dr	21,083	3556	2663
Bel Air				
2402	sedan, 2 dr	62,751	3228	2338
2403	sedan, 4 dr	254,331	3272	2390
2454	sport coupe	166,426	3274	2399
2413	sport sedan	137,672	3336	2464
2434	convertible	47,562	3405	2611
2429	Nomad wagon, 2 dr	6,534	3461	2857
2409	Townsman wagon, 4 dr	27,375	3456	2680

NB All prices, weights, and model numbers for cars equipped with standard V-8 manual transmission.